ANIMAL RESCUE

ANIMAL CONTROL OFFICES

John Clendening

PowerKiDS press.

New York

Published in 2015 by The Rosen Publishing Group, Inc.
29 East 21st Street, New York, NY 10010

First Edition

Produced for Rosen by Cyan Candy, LLC
Editor: Joshua Shadowens
Designer: Erica Clendening, Cyan Candy

Photo Credits: Cover, pp. 5, 7, 8, 9, 11, 15, 16, 17, 21, 25, 27, 29, 30 Shutterstock.com; p. 6 Joelmills, via Wikimedia Commons; p. 12 Habib M'henni / Wikimedia Commons; p. 22 The National Guard, via WIkimedia Commons; p. 23 Delusion23, via Wikimedia Commons.

Library of Congress Cataloging-in-Publication Data

Clendening, John.
 Animal control offices / by John Clendening. — 1st ed.
    pages cm. — (Animal rescue)
 Includes index.
 ISBN 978-1-4777-7019-1 (library binding) — ISBN 978-1-4777-7020-7 (pbk.) —
 ISBN 978-1-4777-7021-4 (6-pack)
 1. Animal welfare—Juvenile literature. 2. Animal shelters—Juvenile literature. I. Title.
 HV4708.C537 2015
 363.7'8—dc23
                                                        2014000015

Manufactured in the United States of America

CPSIA Compliance Information: Batch #WS14PK8: For Further Information contact Rosen Publishing, New York, New York at 1-800-237-9932

TABLE OF CONTENTS

ANIMAL CONTROL OFFICES

Animal control offices provide animal-related services to a community. Most of the services they offer are for animals that people keep as pets, like cats and dogs. Services are also provided to homeless animals.

Unfortunately, there are always homeless animals in every community, so many animal control offices operate animal shelters. Animal shelters provide temporary housing, food, water, and medical care to homeless animals.

In addition to operating shelters, animal control offices offer pet licensing. They also vaccinate and **spay** or **neuter** pets and provide other important services.

Animal control offices are found in almost every community. They are usually operated by cities or counties, but some are operated privately or through public and private partnerships.

It is important for puppies and kittens to receive medical care so they can grow into healthy dogs and cats.

Pets sometimes get lost. If someone loses a pet, a good place to look for it is at the local animal control office. People who find other people's lost animals will often bring the pet to an animal control office. It is the best place to bring a pet that is found.

Animal control offices house the animals that are brought to them until the lost pets can be reunited with their families or find new homes. Animals are provided the shelter and care that they need during their stay.

You can see the small microchip in this X-ray of a dog. Having one placed inside your pet could help you find each other again if your pet ever gets lost.

Animal control officers spend some of their time driving around looking for animals that need help or for animals that have been reported lost by their owners.

Animal Rescue!

Animal control offices may offer microchipping services. A small electronic chip about the size of a grain of rice is injected under an animal's skin without causing the animal pain. If a lost pet is found, the pet's owner can be located and contacted with the information stored on the chip.

WHY COMMUNITIES NEED ANIMAL CONTROL

Animal control offices exist because people and animals live together. We all have to **coexist** safely and peacefully. In the wild, animals survive on what nature provides. **Domesticated** animals have needs that people must provide since they do not live in the wild. Animals living with people rely on care from their owner families. Animals kept as pets do not have to go outside to hunt

This kitten is too young to feed itself. It was brought to an animal control office for help when somebody found it crying and its mother was nowhere to be found.

for food, find water, or find shelter. They have everything they need at home.

Some animals are not so lucky and do not have homes or people to take care of their needs. These animals also live in our communities and some of them can pose a danger to people.

Pets receive medical care from **veterinarians** when they are young. They receive **vaccinations**, or shots, to protect them from diseases as they grow up. Vaccinations also help to prevent animals from making people and other animals sick. Homeless animals that do not receive veterinary care can sometimes be dangerous to people.

If homeless animals have to survive on their own in cities or towns, they may become sick with diseases, such as rabies. If an animal with rabies bites a person, that person could become sick and even die.

Animal Rescue!

Animals do sometimes bite people and can cause serious injuries or even make people sick. If a homeless animal bites you, you must see a doctor right away.

This puppy is getting a checkup from a veterinarian. Veterinarians attend special schools to learn about many different animals so they can help them when they are sick or injured.

ANIMAL CONTROL OFFICERS

Animal control officers work for animal control offices. Their jobs are similar to police officers. Police officers deal with people. Animal control officers respond to calls and requests from people who need help dealing with animals.

Animal control officers do a lot of different things. Some dogs bark too much, and this can annoy neighbors. When a person has a **complaint** about a neighbor's animal, they call animal control. An officer visits with the neighbors to identify the problem and helps to find a solution that makes everybody happy.

Roosters crow to warn other roosters to stay away from them. Roosters are most active in the morning. They have internal clocks that tell them the Sun will be rising soon.

🐾 People in Fairfield, Connecticut, call this cow sculpture Gladys. Gladys is repainted frequently for different events. Here, she was painted to honor a local animal control officer.

Animal Rescue!

Some people like to keep chickens and roosters on their property as pets or to eat their eggs. Roosters can make a lot of noise, especially early in the morning when most people are still sleeping. Under the law, people have the right to enjoy peace and quiet in their homes.

Animal control officers are frequently called on to deal with wild animals like raccoons, opossums, and skunks. These animals often go onto people's property and can cause problems. Officers also **patrol** neighborhoods looking for injured animals that they can help or for pets that people have lost so they can try to reunite them with their families.

Officers also look for homeless animals that can pose a danger to people and bring the animals to a shelter. When the animals are at the shelter, they can receive medical care, and they will not come into contact with people they might hurt. Another important thing these officers do is help animals that are in danger. When natural disasters like floods, hurricanes, or earthquakes happen, sometimes animals need to be rescued just like people do. Animal control officers are also the people who are called to **investigate** when animals bite people.

After driving around looking for animals, animal control officers bring animals back to a shelter so they can be fed and taken care of until their owners find them or until they find homes.

A HISTORY OF ANIMAL CONTROL OFFICES

In the past, most animal control offices were places that homeless, or unwanted were taken so that they couldn't cause harm to people or property. Animals may have been kept there for a few days to see if someone came looking for them. If nobody did, the animals would most often be **euthanized**, or put to sleep.

↑ • Reception
• Pet Adoptions
• Lost and Found
• Animal Intake →

This sign outside an animal control office directs visitors to the services they need. Some offices can be large and have multiple departments.

Animal Rescue!

As populations of people and animals grew, more services were needed to deal with all of the animals. There were more people and animals living together in communities, which increased the chances of dangerous encounters between them. Animal control offices began to expand their services to meet the public's needs.

The focus was more about protecting people from animals than it was about helping animals that needed help. The offices usually did not offer many other services or work toward controlling animal populations as they do today.

During the same time that many people were moving away from rural areas and into cities, it was also becoming more popular for people to keep dogs and cats as pets. In many communities, police departments or health agencies had one animal control officer working for them. As pet populations grew, some communities found that they needed to create new departments to deal only with animals.

After Hurricane Katrina devastated New Orleans in 2005, many people and animals had to be rescued. Animal control officers worked very hard to reunite people with their lost pets.

![paw] Many rescued animals were in urgent need of veterinary care after being injured by Hurricane Katrina. Workers tried to find the animals' owners before putting them up for adoption.

As these new agencies were created, they began to find ways to keep pet populations under control. Some started offering spaying and neutering services. This turned out to be a very successful way to make sure animal populations did not grow out of control. Veterinarians perform these painless operations to make animals **sterile**, or unable to reproduce.

ANIMAL CONTROL OFFICES TODAY

In the past, animals living in animal control offices or shelters were provided only basic care. Today, most animal control offices offer many different services to the public. Many of these services are intended to prevent **overpopulation**, and to keep pets healthy. The offices also educate the public about responsible pet ownership so that people understand the importance of keeping their commitments to take care of their pets for the animals' entire lives.

These services work to promote healthy relationships between people and pets. They also help lower the number of homeless or unwanted animals. Lowering the number of homeless animals makes a community a safer place to live for both people and animals.

Veterinarians check on shelter animals every day to make sure they are healthy. They keep detailed records of animals' health to share with people that come to adopt animals.

Date: 4/7/12
Day Number: ☺
Owner:
Animal: Misty
Breed: Golden Retriever
Admitted:

Vet:
Gender: FN
Age: 4/4/11 3y
Weight:

Clinical Summary:
breeding

Procedures:
None

Called?   Nurse called am: ☑   Vet called: ☐

Fluid therapy   Hartmanns   at   2x   maintena
                              Type of food.
Feeding regime

Medication

Euthanasia is the last resort for animal control offices. When it is necessary to euthanize an animal, it is done with care in a way that ensures the animal feels no pain. It is sad that communities sometimes have to do this, but it gives an animal a peaceful and painless end to what can be a hard, painful, or unsafe life. This is why animal control offices try very hard to get people to **adopt** shelter animals.

There are many military service members living on bases all over the world. They have pets, too. Here a veterinarian who works on a military base examines a kitten.

A sign on this cat's collar tells people the cat has a microchip inside. If this cat gets lost someone can bring it to animal control to help locate its family.

Animal Rescue!

Television is a powerful tool used by animal control offices to get people to adopt shelter animals. In Los Angeles, the county government has a one hundred percent success rate in finding new homes for the one pet it features each week during its televised Board of Supervisors meeting.

ANIMAL CONTROL OFFICES AND SHELTERS WORKING TOGETHER

Most animal control offices operate shelters to care for animals that are brought there. However, that is not the only function of animal control offices anymore. They now serve the public in many different ways.

In some communities there are separate animal shelters that function only to shelter animals without homes. They do not do all the other things that an animal control office often does. Animals are usually brought to an animal control office and then later taken to a separate shelter, if they have no owners or their owners do not claim them. The people who work in these two different places frequently work together to help animals.

These homeless dogs have been put in a crate so they can be transported to an animal shelter. They will have a temporary home there until they can be adopted.

Animal Rescue!

Every day new animals are brought to animal control offices by people who have found them. Sometimes, people who can no longer keep or take care of their pets take them to animal control offices. Animal control officers also bring new animals back to their offices every day after their patrols.

Public shelters operated by animal control offices are often **overwhelmed** by the number of animals they must care. Independent shelters operated by animal welfare organizations will sometimes rescue the animals so they don't have to be euthanized. Unfortunately, at most animal control offices there is not enough space or enough public tax money to take care of all of the animals they serve. Different groups in communities must therefore work together to save animals. Just like people, animals need food and water and a place to live. It all costs a lot of money.

Animal control offices usually deal mostly with dogs and cats, but they also sometimes help take care of other kinds of animals that people keep as pets.

CREATING A BETTER FUTURE FOR ANIMALS

Animal control offices can only do so much with the money available to them. Cities and towns are created by people, for people. Animals that live among us and in our homes need people to help take care of them. Having animal control offices is the main way that society deals with the needs of the many animals living in our communities.

Even though people design cities and towns around the needs of people, pet ownership continues to become more popular each year. Animal control offices continually **evolve** to better serve the needs of the animals with which we share our communities.

Today, shelter animals are often given more space than they once were. They are also given time outdoors to make their lives happier while they stay at a shelter.

Adopting a shelter animal and bringing it home can give an animal a much happier life than it can have in a shelter. People and pets make each other happy.

Animal Rescue!

Animals that live among people in communities cannot earn money to buy their own food or other things they need to survive. Since most cats and dogs do not live in the wild, they cannot survive by hunting as they did before they were domesticated.

Most animal control offices cannot meet the needs of all the animals they serve. Fortunately, there are many people who love animals and help them by operating private shelters. Though, most communities cannot help all the animals that need help, as a society we can improve by working together and becoming more responsible pet owners.

Whether government-run or privately-operated, almost every animal control office or shelter needs help taking care of all of the animals that they rescue. Becoming a **volunteer** is a great way for someone who loves animals to help.

German Shepherd

GLOSSARY

adopt (uh-DOPT) To take something for your own or as your own choice.

coexist (koh-ig-zist) To exist together or at the same time.

complaint (kum-PLAYNT) A statement that something is wrong.

domesticated (duh-MES-tih-kayt-ed) Raised to live with people.

euthanized (yoo-THUH-nihzd) To put an animal to sleep.

evolve (ih-VOLV) To change over many years.

investigate (in-VES-tuh-gayt) To try to learn the facts about something.

neuter (NOO-ter) To fix so that a male animal cannot make babies.

overpopulation (oh-ver-pop-yoo-LAY-shun) To have a population that is so large that it can lead to larger problems, such as environmental or quality of life.

overwhelmed (oh-ver-welmd) To feel overcome by superior force or numbers.

patrol (puh-TROHL) To walk or drive around an area to keep it safe.

spay (SPAY) To fix a female animal so that it cannot have babies.

sterile (STER-ul) Free from germs.

vaccination (vak-shuh-NAY-shun) The act of vaccinating.

veterinarians (veh-tuh-ruh-NER-ee-unz) Doctors who treat animals.

volunteer (vah-lun-TEER) To offer to do something that one does not have to do.

INDEX

WEBSITES

Due to the changing nature of Internet links, PowerKids Press has developed an online list of websites related to the subject of this book. This site is updated regularly. Please use this link to access the list: **www.powerkids.com/ares/offi/**